THE WORLD, FOR YOU

Written by Devaunshi Mahadevia

Illustrated by Sumitra Lokras

For my daughters—

This heart of mine, it beats for you.

May you always know how immensely you are loved,

especially in the quiet spaces between us.

Forever yours,

Mom

My sweet child,

you came into my life

bearing gifts I'd never dreamed of,

and the promise of a love

I had never known before.

In those first few hours we shared,

I, too, made you a promise.

A promise to give you the whole world—

Every wonder the stars can unleash,

Every happiness your heart can hold,

Every bit of love,

collected from the depths of the universe.

Every reason to believe

in the magic of more.

I must admit,

I made those promises

without knowing the weight they would carry,

without understanding the burdens

they would bear for us both.

I didn't tell you

that to give you the whole world

I'd have to go out and gather it

piece by piece,

with gentle hands

and a patient heart.

Sometimes the pieces are messy—
but just like when we begin a new puzzle
we'll pick them up one by one,
make sense of the mess,
and create something beautiful together.

Sometimes the pieces feel unsteady—
but just as we do with the majestic towers you build
that tumble down from time to time,
we will rebuild—
you and me.

I didn't tell you

that there's nothing more I want in this world

than to be by your side,

even when life pulls me in other directions.

June
LAUNDRY

I know that on some days
it all feels a bit unfair.
Your little voice trembles:
"Mom, why can't you just stay a while longer?"

I whisper back,
"I wish I could. Really."

I ache just as deeply as you do
as I peel myself away
from the place my heart feels most at home.

What gives me comfort
is that in those moments apart we grow.

We give each other gifts of a different kind—
Independence. Strength. Courage. Resilience.

Purpose.

"Are you coming back?" you ask.
Worried eyes, a gentle furrow in your brow,
small hands in mine, fingers intertwined—

letting go feels unthinkable.

And I say,

"Of course I'm coming back.
I'll always come back to you."

I'm amazed by how you thrive

in those sunlit hours when I'm away—

collecting stories in the corners of your mind,

creating art,

reading books,

playing pretend,

building castles that we'll live in

forever.

In those moonlit hours

when I return,

you run toward me—

a fireball of love,

stories spilling out with excitement

as you hand me your art on pieces of paper.

"Mom, look, I made these for you!"

you squeal with joy.

I clutch them tight

and absorb them into my being.

Those pages will adorn the walls of my mind

for eternity.

And finally,

in those soon-to-be quiet hours of the night,

I fall asleep next to you—

our fingers again intertwined,

your heart hugging mine,

bringing me back in

to the happiest place I know.

I whisper,

"Didn't I tell you I'd come back?

I will always come back to you."

I'll come back to you

arms cradling

as much of the world

as they can hold—

just for you,

my whole world.

I'll bring back all the pieces I can—

the beautiful and the broken,

the messy and the monumental—

knowing well that you will weave them together

into your own tapestry,

threaded with resolve,

knotted with hope,

and marked by the magic

that is yours alone.

You came into my life

bearing gifts I'd never dreamed of,

and the promise of a love

I had never known before.

And on that day,

I, too, made you a promise—

a promise to give you the whole world,

my whole world

just as you gave me

a whole world

that I had only

ever dreamed of.

NOTES FOR YOUR JOURNEY AHEAD

My Dreams For You

My Wishes For You

My Promises To You

About The Author

Devaunshi Mahadevia is a proud mother and passionate storyteller. Inspired by her daughters, she wrote *The World, For You*—a love letter from parent to child that carries the promise of courage, wonder, and unwavering belonging.

She believes that stories have the power to shape how children see themselves and the world around them. This is her debut children's book and one that will forever hold a special place in her heart.

Devaunshi lives in Connecticut with her husband and their two daughters.